Original title:
Tropical Fruits and Sunsets

Copyright © 2025 Creative Arts Management OÜ
All rights reserved.

Author: Beckett Sinclair
ISBN HARDBACK: 978-1-80586-439-4
ISBN PAPERBACK: 978-1-80586-911-5

Embracing Figs and Fading Light

In the garden, figs hang low,
Bouncing happily to and fro.
A snack for squirrels, quite a treat,
They laugh and dance, oh what a feat!

The sun dips low, a cheeky glance,
As shadows join the evening dance.
We wander round with sticky hands,
These fruits create our silly plans.

With sweet delight, we take a bite,
And giggle as we share our plight.
The juice runs down, a sweet escape,
Our laughter echoes, shaping fate.

As night descends, the stars delight,
We munch our figs, what a sweet sight!
In this embrace, the fun will stay,
Until the dawn takes night away.

Lychee Lullabies and the Twilight Breeze

A lychee ball comes rolling near,
Its fuzzy coat brings childish cheer.
We pop it open, giggles fly,
Sweet laughter rings beneath the sky.

The evening breeze begins to hum,
As playful whispers start to come.
With every bite, the tales unwind,
Of fruity dreams and fun combined.

In twilight's glow, we make a pact,
To chase the snacks, and never act.
With fruity giggles, we unite,
As laughter blends with fading light.

Under stars, we sing our tune,
With lychees round like a big balloon.
In every bite, the pleasures tease,
While swirling with that cheeky breeze.

Glistening Kiwis in the Dimming Glow

Kiwis sparkle like little gems,
In the waning light, oh, what a hem!
We slice them up, green and bright,
Creating chaos in the twilight.

A fruity feast on this warm night,
The laughter bounces, a pure delight.
With every plop, a joke's a-comin',
Our silly antics – oh, they're stunning!

"Let's stick them here," one says with glee,
"Kiwis for eyes—what fun to see!"
And soon we're grinning, quite the sight,
As fruits become our quirky light.

With giggles ringing, we toast our cheer,
To glistening joys, we hold so dear.
In a fruity glow, our night unfolds,
As kiwis shine like tales retold.

The Horizon Sipped Through Mango Straws

Mangoes ripe, like suns that burst,
With every sip, we quench our thirst.
Through straws we slurp, a fruity spree,
Sticky smiles, oh, can't you see?

The horizon blushes, waves of gold,
As tales of sweetness start to unfold.
"More mango!" yells a cheeky child,
Our laughter echoes, dreams run wild.

With every gulp, the giggles grow,
As juice drips down, we steal the show.
We twirl and skip, our joys in tow,
As nightfall paints with a rosy glow.

So raise your straws, let's cheer and sing,
For every mango—what joy they bring!
In this sweet world, we found our way,
With fruity fun to save the day!

Dawn of Guava

The guava smiles in the morning light,
Hiding from squirrels, it jumps with delight.
A cheeky parrot, in a fruity disguise,
Dances with shadows beneath morning skies.

As the sun peeks over the hill,
The guava's plans begin to thrill.
Then out pops a worm, with a grin wide and bright,
Saying, "I promise not to take a big bite!"

Sunset in the Canopy

Up in the trees where the laughter erupts,
Coconuts giggle as they wiggle and thump.
A mango swings by, trying to impress,
But slips on a leaf, oh what a mess!

The sky's painted orange, a colorful show,
While pineapples gossip, not caring to know.
A rambutan shouts, "Look, it's getting late!"
And everyone cheers for the night to cooperate!

A Swaying Lychee Tale

A lychee hung low, playing hide and seek,
As frogs in the pond began to sneak peak.
With a wink from the sun, it beckoned a bee,
"Come dance with me, we can sway with glee!"

The lion fruit laughed, said, "What a weird sight!"
As the lychee spun fast, feeling quite light.
They twirled 'round at dusk, creating a show,
With a chorus of crickets cheering 'go, go, go!'

Carambola Skies

In a field of green, the stars start to fall,
Carambola grins, feeling special and tall.
With rays like a laser, it slices the night,
Beaming at bananas with all of its might.

"I've got this shine, can you handle my flair?"
The bananas respond, "Oh, we don't really care!"
As coyotes howl and the moon takes a dip,
The fruits trade their stories, each sweet little quip.

A Pineapple's Sunset Song

The pineapple wore shades, looking quite cool,
Sipping on juice by the shimmering pool.
A coconut chuckled, floating with grace,
As they watched the sun dance, a bright orange face.

Mangoes joined in, with their fuzzy sweet cheer,
Telling the lemons, "Come over here!"
They formed a conga line on the sand,
Shaking their peels, how hilarious and grand!

Beneath a wide hat, a papaya did sway,
While watermelon seeds planned a grand play.
The sunset was chuckling, a laughing delight,
As the fruits rolled and tumbled into the night.

The Surrendering Sun

The sun yawned loudly, dropping his crown,
As peaches and limes gathered round in the town.
"It's time for a party!" a ripe avocado grinned,
While bananas took bets on the colors he'd send.

A berry brigade marched, all colors and fun,
They chattered excitedly, wishing on the sun.
The oranges squeezed in, trying to boast,
That their zesty glow should be mentioned the most!

Papayas giggled, rolling down hills,
While passionfruit chattered about wild fruit thrills.
As the day bowed out with a wink and a sigh,
All agreed nature knows how to candy the sky!

Lush Harvests and Dreams

In a dream-filled orchard where laughter grew tall,
Grapes threw a rager, inviting them all.
"Cider's on us!" the hard apple called out,
While cherries did cartwheels, creating a route.

With lime and a drizzle, they danced without care,
In the shade of a tree, they sang songs rare.
The sun started slipping, not wanting to leave,
But the fruits teased and tugged, ``Don't you believe?``

When twilight approached with a soft orange glow,
The fruits giggled sweetly, working the show.
With laughter like nectar, the night took its claim,
In this riot of fun, all the fruits knew their name!

The Colorful Farewell

The sky bursts forth in hues so bright,
As birds wear hats and take their flight.
A mango slipped, it cheered a laugh,
While guava danced on the grassy path.

Pineapple jokes, so sharp and sweet,
Tickle the toes of passing feet.
Bananas slide with just a grin,
While oranges roll, let the fun begin!

A papaya sings in the warm breeze,
Tickling the clouds, dancing with ease.
Limes play tag, they're quite the jest,
In this fruity land, we're truly blessed.

The sunset waves, a cheeky chap,
With lemonade dreams, we take a nap.
With laughter echoing, we'll embrace,
This colorful farewell, what a lovely place!

Golden Slices of Daylight

The sun slices through with a wink and a grin,
While coconuts cheer – let the fun begin!
Lemonade rivers flow quick and bright,
As pineapples giggle, they're a pure delight.

A little lime hops on a surfboard,
Sailing through the skies, oh, how he roared!
Tangerines tumble, rolling with glee,
Painting the world in shades of kiwifruit spree.

The day warms up, a banana parade,
Each one a star, in their fruit costume made.
They jive with passion, causing a mess,
Dancing through halos of zestiness.

As daylight fades, still filled with cheer,
Gold slices of laughter, oh so dear.
Let's toast to the sun, and later on, shine,
With fruity giggles, our hearts intertwine!

Melon Mist Over Yonder

A melon mist drifts, soft and light,
As guavas giggle in sheer delight.
The sun winks down, wearing shades of gold,
While Mr. Kiwi narrates tales untold.

Watermelon jokes, they splash like fun,
Tickling sharp tongues, let's all just run!
Mango whispers secrets, sweet and bold,
Underneath palm trees, watch stories unfold.

A fruity riddle hides in the breeze,
Where lychees laugh, and all hearts tease.
Pineapple socks worn low on the wrist,
Play peek-a-boo with the sunset's twist.

So here we sit, with juicy delight,
In this misty wonder, everything feels right.
A party of flavors, fun, and cheer,
Through this radiant world, we'll always steer!

Whispering Palms

Whispering palms sway with a jolly tune,
As star fruits dance beneath the moon.
Crisp cucumber jokes float on air,
While apricots giggle without a care.

Bubblegum skies burst into a laugh,
As cherries play hopscotch, what a gaffe!
The playful breeze tickles the leaves,
With secrets of fruit that the sunset weaves.

A funky coconut wears shades at high noon,
While prickly pears strum a melody soon.
Their great big laughter rings far and wide,
In a world where fruit and fun collide.

Time slows down in this merry bliss,
As flavors and colors perfect a kiss.
With every tick of the day's sweet chime,
We'll dance with joy till the end of time!

The Dream of Ripe Bananas

In pajamas, a banana slipped,
Grinning wide, it did a flip.
It laughed and danced, oh what a sight,
The bunches joined, took flight at night.

A monkey snickered from a tree,
"Is that a dance-off? Come and see!"
They twirled and spun in yellow glee,
While dreams of smoothies floated free.

The moon peeked in, a curious friend,
"Can I join too?" it did descend.
With each twist and every twirl,
The funky fruit made night unfurl.

So when the sun begins to set,
Remember those slips you won't forget.
For laughter hides in every bite,
In dreams of bananas, sweet delight.

Moonlight on Mango Leaves

Moonlight sprinkles mango trees,
They gossip sweetly with the breeze.
"How ripe am I?" one cheeky spoke,
"Let's see who glows like a winking yolk."

The stars just rolled their twinkling eyes,
As mangos blushed in bright disguise.
They dared each other, one by one,
To pull a stunt, let's have some fun!

A clash of colors like a fight,
As orange and green took to the night.
A splash of laughter, juice galore,
Beneath the sky, they danced for sure.

So next time you're under the moon,
Listen closely; hear their tune.
For in the night, they spread their cheer,
Mango parties bring joy near.

Juicy Kisses of Evening

Evening kisses draped in zest,
With pineapples vying for the best.
They wore hats made of coconut shells,
And told wild jokes, oh how they gelled!

Beneath a sky of cotton candy,
Each fruit juggled, feeling dandy.
The lemons laughed till they were sour,
As cherries blushed with floral power.

A splash of color, laughter burst,
The sweetest flavors quenched their thirst.
Strawberries wiggled, playful sprites,
Tickling the air with fruity delights.

So when the sun dips down to rest,
Join this laughter, be a guest.
For juicy fun, it comes alive,
In evening hugs, let flavors thrive.

The Garden of Dusk

In a garden where shadows play,
Fruits come out to dance away.
Pomegranates twirled upon their vines,
While guavas sang in sweet designs.

The papayas giggled, full of cheer,
They pulled the sunset's colors near.
With every step a splash of juice,
They made a mess, what sweet excuse!

Watermelons joined with a plop,
Rolling 'round till each could stop.
The figs were laughing, round and bold,
Sipping dew that never got cold.

As twilight whispers, come and see,
The garden's where they wish to be.
With fruity laughter, bliss in store,
An invitation to dance some more.

Lush Orchards and Fiery Horizons

In orchards ripe, I swung a bat,
Mangoes dodged, they knew I'd splat.
With every swing, a fruit would fly,
Pineapples burst like jokes gone awry.

I danced with fruits, a fruity prance,
Banana peels in a slippery dance.
Beneath the sun, a laughter spree,
Who knew fruit could be so carefree?

As sunlight dipped, the flavors jived,
From watermelon hats, we all derived.
With bursts of juice and zest for fun,
The orchard party had just begun.

So here's to nights with laughs and bites,
Where sunsets blend with fruity delights.
Join me next time when the light's just right,
For an orchard feast and a laugh-filled night.

Sweetness Softened by Dusk

As evening falls, we grab a spoon,
With creamy scoops, we jest and croon.
Mangoes swirl in laughter's chase,
Rhymes of fruit are all over the place!

The coconut's shy, in its leafy wear,
I tried to crack it, but I'm in despair.
Squishy melons chuckle from the side,
"Try again, my friend, it's a wild ride!"

As dusk descends, we melt like ice,
Chocolate sauce makes everything nice.
Pineapples winked in the fading light,
"Chill out, keep smiling, it's all alright!"

Ripening laughter fills the air,
With fruity chaos, we truly dare.
Let's toast to flavors that bring us cheer,
In a sweetened world, we've nothing to fear.

Sun-Kissed Harvests

I skipped through fields, a jester's reel,
Catching guavas, what a steal!
I twirled and laughed, lost in the chase,
A splash of juice, oh what a face!

Avocados rolling, it's quite the sight,
Who knew a fruit could spark such delight?
With each misstep, a giggle breaks,
Fall in a patch? Just more fruit cakes!

The sun paints gold on this fruit parade,
Citrus bubbling, bright escapade.
We squirted juice like little kids,
And somehow, ended with silly bids.

The harvest's done, what a ruckus made,
In every slice, we've unmade the trade.
Let's frolic and feast till the stars come out,
With laughter ringing and fruity shout!

A Symphony of Lychee and Light

A lychee feast, a zany show,
Bouncing around like a fruit ninja pro.
I juggled kiwis, oh what a sight,
It ended in goo, but it felt so right!

The sun dipped low, we sang our tune,
With grapes on hats, we'd dance all afternoon.
"Oh, sunshine, please don't run away,
We've just begun this wild buffet!"

Coconuts rolling, spilled fruit delights,
With laughter and juice, we'll dance through nights.
Be careful, dear friend, don't trip on the peel,
For every fall brings a fruity meal!

As the stars twinkle, we toast our night,
To fruits and joys that always feel right.
With each silly moment, our hearts take flight,
In this light of laughter, all's out of sight.

Endless Horizon of Berry Bliss

On the beach, the mango danced,
With the passion fruit, they pranced.
Pineapple hats on their heads,
Sipping coconut milk in beds.

The sun was laughing in the sky,
As berries tried to learn to fly.
Strawberry shorts and fizzy drinks,
Making mischief, or so it stinks!

Kiwi surfs down a wave so big,
Comes back with a taste of something jig.
Watermelon jokes, so ripe and sweet,
No wonder everyone's on their feet!

At dusk, they all take a break,
Pineapple looks like a big birthday cake.
Lemonade failure sparks a cheer,
The beach is full of fruity cheer!

Dusk's Berry Palette

As the day fades with a funny glow,
Grapefruits gossip, putting on a show.
Bananas slip and giggle with glee,
Dancing shadows, wild and free.

The evening brimmed with laughter bright,
Pomegranates tossing seeds in flight.
Orange slices made a funny face,
While guavas twirled with blushing grace.

Berries rolled like little clowns,
In the sunset's shimmering gowns.
Papaya jokes went soaring high,
Making wave-drum beats in the sky.

When the horizon melted away,
Lychee chuckled, "What a day!"
With laughter echoing in the night,
The fruity fiesta was a delight!

The Echo of an Mango's Pulse

In the grove, where the fruits convene,
A mango's pulse beats strong and keen.
It boasted bright in evening's lace,
Saying, "I'm the life of this place!"

The bananas chimed in, quite absurd,
"A day without laughter, that's unheard!"
Citrus friends all had their say,
Making puns that brightened the way.

As the light began to fade away,
A berry choir began to play.
The rhythm flowed, a juicy beat,
With every laughter, they danced on their feet.

And as night's curtain turned to drop,
Fruits tossed jokes, they couldn't stop.
The echo of laughter so divine,
Fruity hearts all intertwined.

Shadows Among the Lychees

In shadows deep where lychees grin,
Mangoes giggle as the fun begins.
Kiwis whispering secret tales,
While pineapples wear little pails.

The sunset spills a golden hue,
As dragon fruit brings jokes anew.
Ripe berries jostle in playful glee,
"Who's the silliest? Come count to three!"

Their laughter swells like ocean tides,
With every chuckle, the sunset rides.
Grapes rolled by, quite merry and round,
In this fruity dance, joy abounds.

As dusk cloaks them in cozy delight,
The lychee's mischief takes to flight.
With laughter echoing, hearts so free,
In the shadows, all fruits just want to be!

Evening's Palette of Exotic Wonders

Bananas in pajamas swing with glee,
While pineapples dance, so wild and free.
Mangoes giggle with a jolly shout,
As oranges bounce, there's no doubt!

Lychees play hide and seek in the breeze,
With a splash of guavas that aim to tease.
Kiwis in ruffles jump in delight,
As the sun waves goodbye, igniting the night.

Papayas giggle, playing tag on the shore,
While dragon fruit lounges, asking for more.
The sky turns pink with a zesty grin,
Where laughter ripples as the fun begins!

When dusk arrives, it's a fruity dance,
With a twirling star in a bright-colored pants.
Nature paints joy with a vibrant brush,
Under the moonlight, all worries hush.

Ripe Reflection in Dusky Waters

Watermelons float with a sparkle and cheer,
Splashing each other, not a hint of fear.
Cherries are giggling, love in their eyes,
As lemons wiggle, donning sunshine ties.

Coconuts bobble, teasing the shore,
While passion fruits plot for a fruity encore.
A pineapple raps with a beat oh so fine,
While berry buddies sip on fizzy brine.

The sky turns purple, with hues of delight,
As fruits come together to dance through the night.
Reflections of laughter, splashes galore,
In this silly soirée, no one's a bore!

As the stars poke their heads, the moon takes a peek,
Fruits share their secrets, laughter on fleek.
The evening whispers, as the waves softly sway,
In a world full of giggles, they play and they play.

Serenity in a Coconut Shell

Nestled within is a world so round,
Fresh coconut juice makes a splashy sound.
As mangoes debate who wore the best crown,
Papayas sip tea while nobody frowns.

Peachy keen dreams float on yarns of the air,
As turtles munch fruits without a care.
Bananas crack jokes, and lemons just grin,
In this cozy nook, laughter bursts in!

Coconuts chat under the palm fronds,
With berries that twirl to the ocean's song.
Friendship envelopes them, soft as a shell,
With giggles echoing, all's really quite swell.

As the sun dips low, painting skies of gold,
The fruity posse shares tales, bright and bold.
In every warm bubble, joy rings true,
In this coconut haven, friendships renew.

The Raspberry's Gentle Farewell

A raspberry waved, as it rolled down the lane,
Saying goodbye to sunshine, feeling no pain.
Pineapples sighed, wishing for more,
While cherries hooted, causing a roar.

In the orchard of laughter, the fruit brigade met,
Sharing their memories, without a regret.
Grapes slipped on leaves, a clumsy ballet,
While fruit flies cheered in a hilarious way.

The sunset stretched arms, hugging the trees,
While coconuts chuckled, swaying with ease.
With the day fading softly, colors abound,
Each fruit whispered giggles, a treasure they've found.

As twilight cascades, the giggles grow dim,
Yet a raspberry's grin never loses its whim.
In the end, it's clear, fruits know how to play,
With humor in ripeness, they brighten the day.

Golden Skies and Juicy Delights

In the land where pineapples wear hats,
Lemons play tunes, like cheeky little brats.
Coconuts roll down the golden sands,
While silly monkeys form their crazy bands.

Tangerines giggle as they bounce on trees,
Bananas slip-slide, bringing laughs with ease.
A sunset paints laughter in shades of peach,
While fruity shenanigans are just in reach.

Watermelons dance, wiggly and round,
Creating a ruckus, oh what a sound!
Peanut butter jellyfish swim in seas,
As sunbeams tickle every breeze.

With laughter in air, the day bids adieu,
In this fruity circus, the joy feels brand new.
Golden skies chuckle, enjoying the view,
As the world spins in merry, like a sweet brew.

Mango Whispers at Dusk

Mangoes whisper secrets, juicy and sweet,
As they play tag with the warm summer heat.
Strawberries chuckle, hiding in baskets,
Telling tall tales of fanciful caskets.

Candied sunshine kissing on kiwi dreams,
While limey puddles burst into gleams.
The sun does a jig, throws a wink to the sky,
As funky fruit parties begin to fly.

Peaches toss confetti, feeling quite grand,
TikTok bananas do the moonwalk on sand.
Papayas hold hands with the blushing sun,
We're all here for laughs, oh, what fun!

As night spills its ink, they twirl with delight,
Fruit friends all gather, a jubilant sight.
With laughter echoing, a volcano of mirth,
In this fruity fiesta, we're living our worth!

The Papaya's Warm Embrace

A papaya's hug feels oh-so divine,
In a party of colors, tropical and fine.
It snickers and sways, with a jolly good cheer,
Saying, "Life's too short—let's spread joy here!"

Citrusy giggles dance on the breeze,
While cherries give high-fives to the bees.
The sun sets with flair, all shiny and bright,
As fruit cocktails shimmer in the fading light.

Pineapples wear glasses, reading comic strips,
Fruits engaging in giggles and funny quips.
A watermelon chef flips pancakes with flair,
Leaving sticky sweet laughter hanging in air.

As shadows grow long, the fun doesn't fade,
With papaya's embrace, no room for dismay.
Under starry confetti, we share in the glee,
In this fruit-filled haven, we're forever free!

Evening Light on Citrus Dreams

Citrus dreams shimmer in the soft twilight,
Limes doing ballet, looking out of sight.
Oranges juggle stars like it's no big deal,
Evening light winking, oh what a meal!

The tangerine cats chase each other fast,
Delighted they are, they'll have such a blast.
A grapefruit serenades as it strums the breeze,
While zestful laughter pops like fizzy teas.

Berries join in, with a lively parade,
Rolling down hills, all giggles displayed.
Mirth floats in air, like fluff on a cloud,
As coconut trees sway, so cheeky and loud.

With every tick-tock, the joy amplifies,
Under the canvas of raspberry skies.
In this fruity realm, no worries or fears,
Just playful adventures, bringing us cheers!

Silhouettes of the Grove

In a grove where shadows dance,
Lemons play a cheeky prance.
Bananas slip on orange peels,
Laughing loud with joyful squeals.

Papayas in a funny hat,
Swaying like a friendly cat.
Coconuts gossip with delight,
As night rolls in, they hold on tight.

Underneath the leafy shades,
Pineapples throw playful parades.
With every snap of their sweet cheer,
The grove just bursts with pure good cheer.

The Warm Squeeze of Mango

Mangoes squish in sunny rays,
Giggling through the sunlit days.
Juicy drips like laughter flow,
Sticky fingers, what a show!

Peaches join with plump delight,
Chasing shadows on a kite.
Every bite a silly grin,
A fruity dance that won't give in.

Limes do somersaults with flair,
Rolling 'round without a care.
Each sweet scent in the warm breeze,
A fruity feast sure to please!

Serenity in Figs

Figs hang low in calm repose,
Swinging gently, who knows?
Inside secrets, oh so sweet,
With every nibble, a fun treat.

Beneath the sun's warm embrace,
Figs tell tales at a slow pace.
Their laughter echoes through the trees,
Tickling the air like a teasing breeze.

Each round figure, a jolly joke,
Winking under the sunstroke.
In this place where figs unwind,
Happiness is really blind.

A Mirage of Melons

Melons bounce in a bright parade,
Spinning tales of shades they made.
With each slice, they tease and tease,
Juicy smiles that aim to please.

Watermelons in the sun,
Laughing loud, oh what fun!
Cantaloupes play hide and seek,
Giggling softly, cheek to cheek.

Honeydews hum a playful tune,
Beneath the bright and shining moon.
In this mirage, joy will swell,
Fruit-filled laughter rings like a bell.

Under the Fading Foliage

The bananas wear sun hats,
As they gossip by the tree.
Papayas dance in flip-flops,
They're all sipping on sweet tea.

Coconuts roll like laughter,
Joking with the breeze so bright.
A mango's got a punchline,
Underneath the fading light.

Fruits trade their silly stories,
Underneath the glowing sky.
With a voice of the evening,
Each breeze brings a joyful sigh.

As the shadows start to giggle,
And the drizzle starts to cease,
They crack jokes till the moon's up,
In this fruitful tale of peace.

The Nectar of Dusk

Mangoes wear their brightest smiles,
Ripe and ready for the scene.
Pineapples in party hats,
Bobbing in a bowl of green.

Limes crack jokes and poke fun,
While the sunset splashes gold.
Grapefruits giggle in the heat,
Like true jesters, brave and bold.

Citrus fruits are swirling light,
In drinks, they toss their zest.
As the dawn prepares to sleep,
They raise a toast, what a fest!

Nectar drips like merry tunes,
Sweet and silly all around.
With every sip, the world laughs,
In good humor, joy is found.

Blooming at Twilight

A berry blushes with delight,
As the twilight takes a bow.
Kiwi sings with fuzzy charm,
Underneath the boughs, wow!

The oranges play peek-a-boo,
As they sway in evening's glow.
Cherries burst with laughter bright,
Joking with the night's soft flow.

Desserts of juicy whimsy,
Fill the air with fruity cheer.
Each bulging branch a punchline,
To share across the year.

With the stars, the fruits all twinkle,
In the velvet sky's embrace.
They bloom with joy, each moment,
In this funny, sweet ballet.

Pineapple Paradise

Pineapple in shades of gold,
Prances like a festive friend.
With a crown that shouts, 'I'm royal!'
Its laughter seems to extend.

Mangoes roll on sandy shores,
Slipping on their juicy jokes.
Watermelons giggle wide,
With their melodies of yokes.

In this space where sunbeams play,
And fruits swing like a parade,
Peaches waltz on ocean waves,
In the laughter that they've made.

As the night begins to fall,
Citrus sparks the air with cheer,
Each fruity friend in harmony,
In this paradise we hold dear.

The Banana Grove at Sundown

In a grove where bananas sway,
Monkeys dance and laugh all day.
They slip and slide with sunny glee,
Who knew fruits could climb a tree?

The sunset paints the sky so bright,
While fruit flies hum a silly flight.
A coconut falls, it lands with a thud,
Watch out below, it's a bouncy flood!

Pineapples wear their crowns with pride,
While avocados roll like they've got nothing to hide.
A parrot jokes, "Don't eat me, please!"
While mangoes giggle in the breezy tease.

"Let's throw a party, come join the fun!"
Said the durian; it stinks, but he's number one.
The fruit bowl's ready, friends all around,
In this sunshine, there's laughter unbound!

Vibrant Hues of Coral and Lime

A lime rolled down the fervent hill,
It met a coral, both full of thrill.
Dancing together, they spun in delight,
A citrus tango under the fading light.

The sunset drips, oh what a sight,
Pink and orange, with a dash of fright!
A parsnip peeked, said, "What's that glow?"
The lime replied, "Just a sunset show."

A grapefruit shouted, "I want in too!"
As colors mixed, a vibrant hue.
They giggled and bounced, what a silly crew,
As finding their flavors became quite the to-do.

"Let's paint the town with zest so bright,"
Cried mangos and guavas in pure delight.
With laughter and joy, they filled the air,
In this carnival realm, none had a care!

Nectarine Skies and Ocean Breezes

The ocean sings a fruity tune,
Where nectarines sway beneath the moon.
A peach chimed in, "I'm ripe for the night!"
As coconuts rocked in sheer delight.

The waves crashed down with a giggle and splash,
While cherries bounced in a sandy dash.
"Surf's up!" called a wayward lime,
As laughter rolled in like sweet sunshine.

The sea was a party, so fresh and bold,
With jellybeans dancing, a sight to behold.
Bananas in boats, sailing carefree,
Becoming legends of the salty spree.

"Hey, who wants a pie?" shouted a fig,
But the mango just giggled, "You're way too big!"
With nectarines glowing in the ocean's sway,
Silly moments turned night into day!

Apricot Dreams Beneath Starlit Canopies

Underneath a starry dome,
Apricots dream of a far-off home.
With giggles and whispers among the leaves,
They spin tales that nobody believes.

The night air hums with fruity praise,
And the grapefruits dance in a silly daze.
"Hey look, that star is a jellybean!"
They laugh and twirl, it's quite the scene.

A rascal berry tried to take flight,
But ended up stuck in a peach's sight.
"Help me out, it's a fruity mess!"
Cried the berry with comical distress.

"The dream is real, let's make it last,
We'll cover the cosmos with our fruity blast!"
With laughter blending in the airy bliss,
Each starlit story became pure happiness!

The Fruitful Embrace

In the orchard where the guava grows,
Mangoes dance in silly rows,
Pineapple wears a crown so grand,
While coconuts roll like they just can't stand.

Bananas slip and take a dive,
Chasing limes that feel so alive,
Papayas giggle, ripe and bright,
Waving goodbye to the fading light.

Fruit flies buzz like they own the place,
While oranges jive in a citrus chase,
And don't forget the plums that prance,
Born to join this fruity dance!

With every bite, each flavor's a tease,
Laughter fills the fragrant breeze,
As we savor this playful feast,
In a world where joy has never ceased.

Banjan Boughs and Remnants of Day

Underneath the bending boughs,
Where lemons lounge and limes make vows,
Kiwi flies on a sunny whim,
Teasing everyone with a little grin.

The sun sinks low, a peachy blur,
While cherries giggle and start to stir,
A mango winks like it's in on a joke,
Its juicy secret, not even a poke!

Papaya plays hide-and-seek with the stars,
While berries plot their sweet memoirs,
Vines twist like they're tipsy from fun,
As laughter echoes with the setting sun.

Each fruit swings from goofy trees,
Whispering secrets on the breeze,
The day hugs night, a comical embrace,
In this fruity and fun-filled place.

Papaya Lanterns

Hanging low like lanterns bright,
Papayas laugh at the coming night,
Bouncing softly on the breeze,
Just like jokes meant to tease.

Under the glow of a glowing star,
Coconuts giggle, shouting "We're bizarre!"
While watermelons have a party hat,
Inviting everyone for a playful chat.

Pineapples dance in a silly line,
Swaying gently, oh so fine,
And if you listen close enough near,
You'll hear them whisper, "We've got no fear!"

As the night unfolds with fruity cheer,
With happiness spun from every sphere,
This orchard's joy will never wane,
As laughter mingles with the moonlit gain.

Evening Harvest

As twilight falls upon the grove,
The harvest sings, sweet tones to rove,
Limes wear hats made of fluffy fluff,
While cherries shout, "We can't get enough!"

Ripe figs are hiding, holding tight,
As oranges giggle at the fading light,
Glancing sideways with a cheeky grin,
Shouting, "When does the fun begin?"

Persimmons roll in a playful spree,
Bananas cheer, "Come join, oh please!"
With every bite, they find delight,
Creating laughter, pure and bright.

As night drapes a blanket of stars,
The fruits conspire, plotting their bars,
A riotous feast of joy-filled hearts,
In the whimsical world of fruity arts.

Papaya Rain and Sunset Stains

When papayas drop from trees so high,
The squirrels giggle, oh my, oh my!
Splashing juice while no one sees,
They dance away on sticky knees.

The sun dips low, a golden ball,
A slice of amber, we all call.
But watch your toes, it's quite the game,
With every step, it's papaya shame!

The clouds turn pink, a berry dream,
While birds chirp loudly, join the scheme.
They wave their wings, in sunset's glow,
While squirrels plan their next big show.

And as the night takes over bright,
The stars will laugh, oh what a sight!
With every fruit that falls beside,
We celebrate, take it in stride.

Embracing Each Day's Fermented Sweetness

Each morning brings a vat of cheer,
Fermented joy just waiting near.
With laughter bubbling in our mugs,
We toast to life, to fruity hugs!

The guava giggles, the limes conspire,
A zesty dance around the fire.
Let's drip and drop, no need for care,
As sticky juice fills all the air!

When evening falls, the stars come out,
We wonder what this fuss is about.
Like berries tossed in a silly fight,
We bounce and roll until it's night.

So raise your glass, let's share a grin,
With every sip, we let joy in.
Sweetness lingers, the fun won't end,
In our fruity world, big laughs we send!

Golden Horizon

The sun peeks out, a golden fold,
It warms the hearts, the glee unfolds.
With laughter bright, the day ignites,
We chase the rays, in playful flights.

Beneath the palms, we find our place,
As fruit spills out in a fine disgrace.
Bananas slip and mangoes tease,
With every step, we squeal with glee!

Oh, what a sight, the sky ablaze,
As day turns night in citrus haze.
We weave our tales with a splash of zest,
In this banana boat, we're truly blessed!

The colors swirl, a fruity fight,
In sunset's arms, it feels so right.
Tomorrow calls, let's dance again,
In endless loops, our fruity friend.

Mango Whispers

Oh, mangoes whisper in the breeze,
With secret tales that tease and tease.
They tickle noses, make you grin,
A funny game where we all win!

As sunsets pour their golden syrup,
The fruit parade is quite the stirrup.
We juggle limes, take a goofy stance,
As every drop ignites a dance.

With laughter woven in the air,
The berries shout, "Life's not unfair!"
From every slice, we spread the glee,
With fruity jokes, we sing with glee.

So when the night creeps in with flair,
Don't let that joy dissolve in air.
We'll toast to fun, to laughter's reign,
In every fruit, we find our gain.

Sunset in the Grove

In the grove where shadows play,
Mangoes giggle at the end of day.
Pineapples wear a golden crown,
While coconuts politely drown.

Lemurs swing, they dance and twirl,
One slips and gives the breeze a whirl.
Papayas bounce like they're on a spree,
Who knew they'd steal the show so free!

As the sun dips, colors rise,
Bananas grinning, oh what a surprise!
They juggle berries in a cheerful race,
While oranges roll and steal their place.

The Lure of Lime

Lime, oh lime, your zest is bright,
A ball in a bowl, what a silly sight!
You dance on the table, green and round,
Chasing laughter, making no sound.

Lemonade dreams in the evening haze,
With a twist of a slice to brighten the phase.
I'm telling jokes, they're laughing too,
Even the limes are turning blue!

Salt on the rim, what else can we find?
Pineapples snicker, they'll give you a grind.
Oh, fruity friends in a jolly fate,
Here in the bowl, we all relate!

Ripe Echoes of Serenity

Under the shade, ripe fruits conspire,
Each with a tale that will never tire.
Guavas gossip about the day's fun,
While jackfruits fumble, oh what a run!

The sun whispers secrets, oh so shy,
Avocados giggle, saying goodbye.
While cherries play dodge with a breeze so light,
We all sit back, what a hilarious sight!

With every bite, a burst of cheer,
Citrus chuckles filling the atmosphere.
Underneath the stars, a fruit feast awaits,
As laughter unites, so love reverberates.

Evening Bliss Among the Trees

In the stillness, laughter rings,
As laughter flies on the back of wings.
Fruits hang low, they join the fun,
Bouncing berries under the setting sun.

Kiwi giggles, flipping on a vine,
Passion fruits waltz, isn't it divine?
Beneath the palms, we're all aglow,
As laughter ripples, oh what a show!

Night creeps in, the stars align,
Fruits with dreams that intertwine.
We raise a toast to nature's jest,
In this playful orchard, we feel blessed.

Grapefruit Glow

In the morning light, so bright and bold,
A zesty orb, it's worth its weight in gold.
I squeezed it tight, oh what a sight,
  My face, a twist, a funny delight.

My breakfast dance, a citrusy prance,
With grapefruit slices, I take a chance.
The juice it splashed, a comical fate,
  I wore my snack while feeling great.

Peeled and pitted, oh what a mess,
  An orange escape, I must confess.
But laughter bubbles like a fizzy brew,
In grapefruit glow, my joy breaks through.

As parched as sand, I take a plunge,
  With every bite, I start to grunge.
  My fruit parade, a cheerful kin,
  In this sunny time, let the fun begin!

Sunset's Ripe Farewell

As the day retreats, a peachy tease,
The sky transforms, a sight to please.
A giggle erupts, as colors clash,
Pink and orange in a daily splash.

Bananas hanging, swaying with flair,
As blushing berries declare, 'We care!'
A fruity farewell, so chubby and grand,
The sun waves goodbye with a sun-kissed hand.

Mangoes pirouette in the amber glow,
And I can't help but steal the show.
With every munch, a juicy delight,
The sunset's ripe, what a fruity night!

Limes laugh too, in this vibrant scene,
While coconuts dance, oh so keen.
Fruits spinning tales, in sunset's spell,
With a cheeky grin, I wish them well!

The Orchard's Lullaby

In an orchard bright, the fruits sing loud,
Tomatoes blush, oh they're so proud.
An apple's giggle, a merry round,
While cherries chuckle, blissfully bound.

Yes, here they sway, all right on cue,
With jokes and jests, they're never blue.
A peach tells tales of sweltering days,
While lemons roll in their zesty ways.

A banana slips, in a jovial spree,
As laughter spreads from tree to tree.
Coconuts rock, in harmony they sway,
Singing lullabies till the break of day.

The harvest brings joy, cut fresh and sweet,
Crunching and munching, a treat to eat.
In the orchard's embrace, we dream in delight,
Savoring memories, a magical night!

Cacao Dreams

In a world of sweetness, where beans collide,
A cacao bean rolls, with laughter inside.
With dreams of chocolate, oh what a thrill,
I chuckle away, sip cocoa at will.

Milk froths high, a cappuccino twist,
As marshmallows dance, I can't resist.
Frothy delights, my giggles abound,
Cacao fantasies swirl all around.

As I sip slowly, the world turns bright,
With every taste, it feels just right.
Dark or milk, it's a joyous scheme,
In cacao dreams, I chuckle and beam.

So raise a cup, let the good times flow,
In this chocolate world, let merriment grow.
With every sip, a funny cue,
Cacao and laughter, the perfect brew!

Coconut Dreams at Dusk

In a hammock swaying, I sip my drink,
Coconut whispers make me think,
Of a parrot who danced on a lime,
Chasing his shadow, oh what a crime!

Underneath palm leaves, I spot a crab,
Wearing sunglasses, looking fab,
He prances and dances with great flair,
I can't help but giggle, what a rare pair!

As the sun dips low, I munch a mango,
Sticky fingers, oh, what a tango!
The juice trickles down, sweet and bright,
Like a sunset painted in pure delight!

So here I lay with my fruity friends,
Wishing this laughter never ends,
Sippin' and laughin' with a pinch of grace,
In this sunset paradise, we find our place.

Starfruit Starlight

Star-shaped treasures hang from the tree,
A fruit that winks at you and me,
I took a bite, and the juice burst bright,
Made me dance under the moonlight.

Bananas giggle as they peel away,
Spelling secrets in the light of day,
Pineapple crowns, so proud and tall,
Swaying their leaves in a silly sprawl.

Beneath the stars, papayas join the fun,
Telling tales of how they once spun,
A contest of who can roll the best,
Those fruity shenanigans put to the test!

With a chuckle, I watch the display,
As fruit and laughter dance and sway,
Underneath a sky all glittery and bright,
Silliness reigns in the starlit night.

Sunset Juxtaposition

A berry's blush meets a soft orange hue,
As the sky paints itself just for you,
A lime starts cracking jokes above,
While the oranges blush with a hint of love.

The sunset grins, slapping on some pink,
With a cheeky wink, what do you think?
A chorus of flavors begins to sing,
Catching the laughter that night will bring.

Watermelon giggles with each little bite,
It's a slippery slope under the twilight,
As I juggle fruits in a comedic spree,
The stars chime in, "You look silly, tee-hee!"

In this patch of color where laughter grows,
Bananas in tuxedos strike a pose,
With each sunset splash, a grin so wide,
Keep the chuckles coming, let's enjoy the ride!

Frangipani and Fruit

Frangipani dreams dance in the breeze,
As juicy surprises try to tease,
A cherry crossed paths with a fruit bat,
Now they giggle—imagine that!

Lychees in the shade, wearing hats so fine,
Regaling the fruits over sips of wine,
"Mango, you're famous!" cries out the cantaloupe,
As they all burst forth, teeming with hope!

Avocado's secret: a pit for a twin,
He's on a vacation, enjoying the din,
While coconuts chuckle, all round and stout,
Curious critters poke and shout!

In this carnival of flavors, joy explodes,
With laughter echoing down the roads,
Let's toast to the fun, the fun we create,
With frangipani blooms that can hardly wait!

Hues of Midnight

The sky turned pink, like a drink gone wrong,
A mango slipped, danced to the song.
Bananas wore shades, all cool and bright,
While coconuts giggled, what a funny sight.

Papayas and guavas, my friends in the shade,
All plotting mischief, in bright masquerade.
With laughter and sighs, the stars join the fun,
As pineapples roar, 'This night has begun!'

The limes roll about, a zesty parade,
While oranges juggle, in a citrus charade.
We toast to our shenanigans under the glow,
With smiles far bigger than the moon's soft show.

So raise up your glass to this fruit-filled night,
Where dreams and vitamin C take flight.
In this wild fruit kingdom, we frolic and play,
As the night whispers secrets, 'Come join the fray!'

Pineapple Porches

On porches of pineapples, we swing and sway,
While coconut cookies try to roll away.
Mangoes tell stories of far-off shores,
As kiwis debate what it means to be poor.

The sun gets sleepy, painting skies in gold,
Grapefruits gossip, their stories retold.
Chocolate bananas, in pajamas, parade,
While we laugh at the jokes that the apples have made.

A fruitcake erupts in a burst of delight,
With cherries all winking, the mood is just right.
We devour the sunshine, sip nectar from cups,
As late-night desserts join to fill us with ups.

So pull up a seat on this porch made of cheer,
Where every bite's silly, and laughter is near.
Hats off to the fruits, in their bright, zesty sprawl,
For under this moon, we are one and all.

Lush Reflections

In the garden of giggles, ripe laughter grows,
With watermelons blushing, striking silly poses.
Berries in bow ties, they dance on the grass,
While cherries in circles invite us to pass.

The pineapple whispers witty puns with glee,
As the papaya grins, 'Just wait and see!'
Bananas slip on, adding flair to the night,
While kumquats sing softly, 'Everything's right.'

In pools of sunshine, the stars try to shine,
Twinkling like fruits that just crossed the line.
With laughter reverberating through leaf and vine,
This lush, fruity madness feels utterly fine.

So gather your friends, let the revelry flow,
Where joy is the fruit, and it's all for show.
Under this canopy of delight and fun,
We dance till the morning, 'til twilight is done.

The Citrus Cascade

In a waterfall, oranges take their dive,
Dancing like children, so bright and alive.
Lemons giggle and splash, oh what a sight,
As the grapefruits tumble, full of delight.

Tiny limes zoom by, racing for a crown,
While pomelos stand tall, never feeling down.
Kiwi kites float, bright green in the sun,
As juicy mangoes cheer, 'Oh, let's have some fun!'

A cascade of flavors, so fresh and so bold,
With laughter as vibrant as the sunshine they hold.
Pineapples swoosh by on a surfboard of zest,
Proclaiming, "This splash party is simply the best!"

So let's join the flow, in this juicy parade,
Where every bright color crafts laughter displayed.
In this citrus explosion, the joy never fades,
We savor the moments, as our fun brigade wades.

The Last Squeeze of Day

The sun drops low in a zesty glow,
Oranges giggle as they start to show.
Pineapples dance with a tipsy breeze,
In a fruit parade that's sure to please.

Lemons squeeze jokes as they roll on by,
A coconut laughs, oh my oh my!
With watermelon seeds all over the place,
Bananas slip in a race for space.

Kiwi pulls up for a grand ol' time,
Cherries chuckle, all in their prime.
The day waves goodbye, what a fruity affair,
As the night comes in, they just don't care!

Fruit pies are devoured, the laughter's a blast,
With the last squeeze of day, we're having a blast!

Tropical Chill

Under the sun, a mango reclines,
In shades made of leaves, sipping fine wines.
Papaya giggles, "What a lazy day!"
As lychee whispers, "Let's just play."

Coconuts roll, in a silly race,
Carved into hats, they don't mind the space.
With each little giggle, a coconut sighs,
"Life's just a fruit bowl, look how it flies!"

Melons join in with their sweet, juicy jive,
While oranges throw slices, just to survive.
"Do you feel the rhythm?" a passion fruit sings,
As the sun dips low and the laughter clings.

With laughter and juice, we dance till we drop,
In this fun-filled chill, we just can't stop!

Papaya Tango

In the shade, a papaya starts to twirl,
With a passion fruit, they twist and swirl.
Together they laugh, what a fruity dance,
As pineapples cheer, "Give it a chance!"

Limes get zesty, taking the lead,
While durian jokes sparkle with heed.
"What's that smell?" a mango teases,
"Oh, it's just me!" the durian pleases.

With each little step, they hop and sway,
Avocado joins in, calling, "Hooray!"
Bananas slip in, but with style and grace,
Remembering always to keep up the pace.

At the end of the night, they bow with flair,
The fruit tango wraps up with a shared stare,
To dance and to laugh, what a zesty charade,
In a world of colors, their dreams cascade.

The Cascade of Evening

As the light starts to fade, berries unite,
To chat about life and the stars shining bright.
"Did you see that? A banana took flight!"
They chuckle and snicker, what a silly sight.

The evening cascades with mango moonbeams,
While papayas sip dreams filled with sweet creams.
"Let's throw a party!" sings a ripe little fig,
And the whole fruity crew does a hilarious jig.

Dates roll on in with an offer so sweet,
"Let's dance till we drop and get off our feet!"
With cookie crumbs flying and laughter galore,
They munch on their treats, "More fruit, just encore!"

As the stars twinkle and the laughter flows,
This fruity soirée just perfectly glows.
With every sweet moment as night drifts away,
They dance in the moonlight until the first ray.

Passionfruit Serenade

In the garden, fruits collide,
With seeds that dance like they're on a ride.
A wrinkled face with a flavor to boast,
Passionfruit giggles, it's the brunch-time toast.

Juice drips down like a sunshine rain,
Lemonade hopes it can share the fame.
But all eyes are on the jelly-like orb,
As it wobbles and bounces, ready to absorb.

The squirrels peek in with a cheeky grin,
"Is this fruit party? We're ready to win!"
Boys with straws have gathered the crowd,
Taking sips of love, laughing out loud.

As twilight nears, the laughs take flight,
With passionfruit jokes that last through the night.
The starry sky blushes in shades of glee,
While everyone dances, buzzing with free.

Sunset Melodies over Pineapple Fields

Pineapples sway in the evening glow,
Like hula dancers, in a fruity show.
The golden crowns, they shimmer and shine,
Each twist and turn makes the day divine.

Laughter bounces through rows of delight,
As we sip mocktails, oh what a sight!
With every slice and every squish,
We make a toast, 'Oh, what a dish!'

A cloud-shaped like a fruit flies by,
"Pineapple fritters!" we hear someone cry.
But it's just the sunset, painting the sky,
As giggles erupt, nobody asks why.

The fields are alive with the buzz and cheer,
As pineapples whisper, "We're glad you're here!"
The music of nature, we sway with the breeze,
Creating our fun, like thieves with the cheese.

Guava Glow in Twilight's Arms

Guavas hide in the foliage green,
With rosy cheeks, they're the sweetest seen.
Each bite is a giggle, a crunchy surprise,
As we savor their fun with wide-open eyes.

The twilight wraps softly around our spree,
With guava games played by neighborly bees.
"Is that a fruit? Or a fuzzy delight?"
The answers come forth, buzzing all night.

We slice and we munch, bursting with fun,
Trading our giggles, one by one.
Our glasses are full, sticky with juice,
As the fireflies tune in, no need for a truce.

The world holds its breath, in the soft twilight,
As guavas glow pink, making everything right.
With laughter as fruit, we toast with a cheer,
And dance through the night, with the stars drawing near.

The Last Mango of Summer

Oh, the last mango shines so bright,
As summer waves its final goodbye.
With a wink from the sun, and a twist of fate,
We gather around, it's a sweet, juicy date.

Ripe and ready, it slips from our hands,
Landing soft like a clap of bands.
"Mango tango!" we all start to sing,
As it rolls and twirls, it's a magical thing.

The bees start to buzz, giving some flair,
"Don't worry, dear friends, we don't have a care!"
With each creamy slice, laughter ignites,
We dream of mango shenanigans all night.

As the sunset bids, we hold on tight,
To the last mango, our summer delight.
With sticky fingers, we'll never forget,
How laughter and sweetness hold hands with sunset.

A Dance of Shadows and Silken Fruits

In the breeze, a coconut sways,
A parrot mocks the sun's blaze.
Under palm fronds, laughter we hear,
As mangoes fall, it's a fruity sphere.

Bananas peek from leafy piles,
While limes roll down the aisles.
Oh, what mischief fruits can make,
In the evening light, we all partake.

Papayas giggle as they hide,
Behind the branches, full of pride.
A pineapple juggles, oh what a sight,
While we're all basking in golden light.

Grapefruits dance with stylish flair,
Adding zest to the sun's glare.
Jokes are shared, and songs are sung,
In this fruity realm where fun is flung.

The Last Rays on Jackfruit Trees

At dusk, the jackfruit's shadow grows,
While kids play tag in soft, warm throes.
Peeling back the orange skin,
A tasty treat lies deep within.

Laughter bubbles, as kids do prance,
Around the trees, it's a wacky dance.
With sticky hands and sticky feet,
We munch on fruit, oh what a feat!

The sun dips low, we start to cheer,
For every jackfruit pie this year!
We'll bake and laugh with no regrets,
While dodging bees and sticky pets.

As night descends, we toast our dreams,
With fruity drinks and giggly beams.
Oh, the tales we'll share, the joy we seize,
Under the spell of jackfruit trees.

Colorful Echoes of Golden Hour

The sky ablaze, a splash of cheer,
As fruit confetti draws us near.
Kiwi slices dance in a bowl,
While sunset colors steal the show.

Pineapple wigs blow in the breeze,
Strutting around with fruity ease.
Laughter flies like birds in flight,
As currants twirl in wicked delight.

Beneath the sky, we sip and laugh,
Splitting coconuts in our behalf.
Strawberries giggle, such juicy sights,
In this party of juicy delights.

As the hues melt, we sing our tune,
With friends and fruits beneath the moon.
For every taste, a joyful cheer,
In this colorful hour, we hold dear.

Sunset Brewed in Cacao Bliss

In the evening, cocoa swirls,
While fondue pots begin to twirl.
A marshmallow catwalk makes us grin,
As chocolate rivers start to spin.

Strawberry boats on the cocoa sea,
Sailing home from a giggly spree.
Bananas scoop the creamy snacks,
While laughter flows like sweet, rich tracks.

Caramel clouds hang low and round,
While sweet aromas dance around.
We take a dip, a sugary dive,
As carefree spirits soar alive.

With each scoop, a chuckle shared,
In this bliss, no one is spared.
For in chocolate we find pure joy,
As silly as a playful toy.

Lychee Light

In a market bright, oh what a sight,
Lychees in piles, oh what a delight!
They wink and they giggle, a fruity parade,
Beneath brown paper bags, their plans well laid.

A little old man in a straw hat,
Sips on a drink with a cheeky chat.
"One's for the heart, two's just for fun,
But don't mix with mango, that's no good run!"

With every sweet bite, a burst of cheer,
Juices so slippery, they bounce, I fear!
Girls in bright dresses, they dance by the stand,
While giggling fruits plot to rule the land.

Under this canopy, the sunshine beams,
With laughter and joy, we chase our dreams.
So grab your fancy hats and take a crash,
Sip on some joy, then off for a splash!

Bananas in the Breeze

Have you ever seen a banana in flight?
Swinging on branches, oh what a sight!
They chat with each other in playful tease,
"Catch me if you can!"—they laugh in the breeze.

As they bounce and they sway, they swirl all around,
Wiggling their peels on the fun fruit ground.
One said to a mango, "Do you feel that breeze?
It's my banana charm, darling, watch me tease!"

The sun starts to dip, what a golden glow,
Bananas wear shades, and their smiles grow.
With party hats on and drinks made of rum,
They host a wild bash, and oh, what a fun!

As night falls around, there's laughter and sound,
The peels dance together, joy unbound.
So join in the fun, don't worry 'bout spills,
With bananas around, you'll get all the thrills!

Sunset Fragrance

When the sky sings gold, and colors collide,
A fruit basket spills by the ocean's side.
Coconuts whisper tales of the sea,
While limes in the corner giggle with glee.

Pineapples strut with a swagger so bold,
Their juice is the story that never gets old.
"I may be spiky, but I'm sweet as can be,
How about a slice? I'm the life of the spree!"

The curtain of night slowly drapes the bay,
Starfruit overhead joins in the play.
Grapefruits gossip of love from above,
While berries say, "Hey, can we talk of love?"

With scents in the air that tickle the nose,
Passion fruits pulse where the soft wind flows.
So grab a fruit friend, let the laughter blend,
Tonight's fruity saga will never end!

Hibiscus and Horizon

A hibiscus bloom with a sparkly grin,
Sips nectar from petals—let the day begin!
"I'm the flower queen, take a look, so fine!
But watch out for bees, they want to dine!"

Nearby, a coconut's doing a jig,
He shakes and he rolls, thinks he's quite big.
"Hey, blossom, my dear, join me for fun!
Together we'll shine as bright as the sun!"

As the horizon blushes in hues of delight,
The fruits start to twirl in magical flight.
Jackfruits join in, with a thump and a clap,
Making a scene that brings joy—it's a wrap!

With laughter and color in perfect embrace,
We dance through the gardens, a vibrant place.
So plant your own seeds of joy and surprise,
Watch nature's big show right before your eyes!

www.ingramcontent.com/pod-product-compliance
Lightning Source LLC
Chambersburg PA
CBHW060139230426
43661CB00003B/481